UNDERSTANDING GAMERS
THE COLLECTED DORK TOWER, VOLUME V

By John Kovalic

DORK STORM PRESS

OTHER BOOKS BY JOHN KOVALIC

Dork Covenant: The Collected Dork Tower Volume I
(Issues 1-6 of the comic book)

Dork Shadows: The Collected Dork Tower Volume II
(Issues 7-12 of the comic book)

Heart of Dorkness: The Collected Dork Tower Volume III
(Issues 13-17 of the comic book)

Livin' la Vida Dorka: The Collected Dork Tower Volume IV
(previously uncollected comic strips from national magazines and dorktower.com)

Understanding Gamers: The Collected Dork Tower Volume V
(Dork Tower 18, the Lord of the Rings special, plus previously uncollected comic strips)

1d6 Degrees of Separation: The Collected Dork Tower Volume VI
(Issues 19-24 of the comic book) (Autumn 2003)

Crouching Weasel, Hidden Muskrat: The Collected Wild Life Volume I
(Wild Life comic strips from college to national syndication) (Spring 2004)

DORK STORM PRESS
PO Box 45063
Madison, WI 53744
http://www.dorkstorm.com

Marketing, sales and advertising inquiries
sales@dorkstirm.com

Editorial and other inquiries
john@kovalic.com

Interior design and layout: Jeff Mackintosh

PRINTED IN THE USA • FIRST PRINTING • JUNE 2003 * ISBN 1-930964-47-1

WIL WHEATON DOT NET
50,000 monkeys at 50,000 typewriters can't be wrong

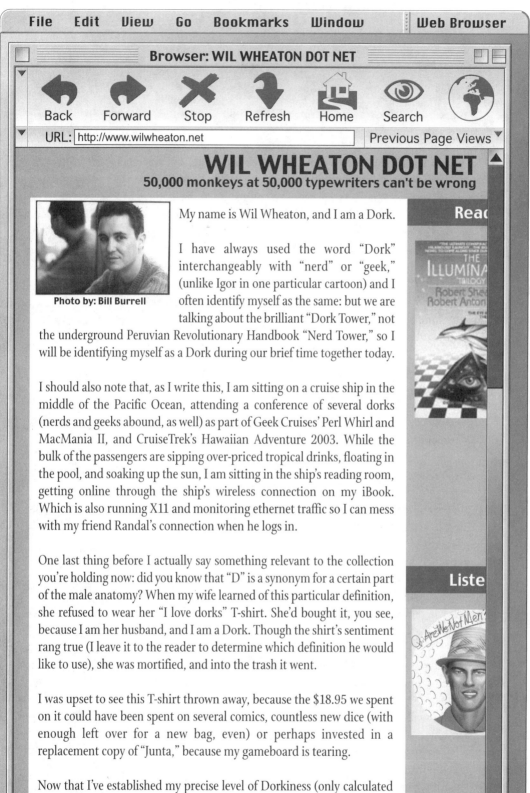

Photo by: Bill Burrell

My name is Wil Wheaton, and I am a Dork.

I have always used the word "Dork" interchangeably with "nerd" or "geek," (unlike Igor in one particular cartoon) and I often identify myself as the same: but we are talking about the brilliant "Dork Tower," not the underground Peruvian Revolutionary Handbook "Nerd Tower," so I will be identifying myself as a Dork during our brief time together today.

I should also note that, as I write this, I am sitting on a cruise ship in the middle of the Pacific Ocean, attending a conference of several dorks (nerds and geeks abound, as well) as part of Geek Cruises' Perl Whirl and MacMania II, and CruiseTrek's Hawaiian Adventure 2003. While the bulk of the passengers are sipping over-priced tropical drinks, floating in the pool, and soaking up the sun, I am sitting in the ship's reading room, getting online through the ship's wireless connection on my iBook. Which is also running X11 and monitoring ethernet traffic so I can mess with my friend Randal's connection when he logs in.

One last thing before I actually say something relevant to the collection you're holding now: did you know that "D" is a synonym for a certain part of the male anatomy? When my wife learned of this particular definition, she refused to wear her "I love dorks" T-shirt. She'd bought it, you see, because I am her husband, and I am a Dork. Though the shirt's sentiment rang true (I leave it to the reader to determine which definition he would like to use), she was mortified, and into the trash it went.

I was upset to see this T-shirt thrown away, because the $18.95 we spent on it could have been spent on several comics, countless new dice (with enough left over for a new bag, even) or perhaps invested in a replacement copy of "Junta," because my gameboard is tearing.

Now that I've established my precise level of Dorkiness (only calculated to within .005, because I don't have any graph paper on me), let's get to the actual introduction, shall we? Excelsior!

Internet Zone

This is a book about me. It's probably a book about you, and several of your friends, and lots of people just like us, too. We know who we are: we camped out for Star Wars Episode One, and still haven't bothered to watch Episode 2 on DVD, lest we get burned again. We have signed the petition to remind future generations that GREEDO SHOOTS FIRST! We have hundreds of polyhedral dice, but we only use eight of them, and those are kept in their own special bag. (Mine is a black velour bag, with the symbol for the Bavarian Illuminati stamped onto it in red. My dice are all black with red numbers, except for my d20's, which are clear with black numbers. I also have 2 d6's which have skulls where the number one should be . . . but I rarely use them. They're mostly there for effect.)

If you're One of Us, you'll cackle as you read these pages, because there isn't a false word or drawing here. If you're One of Us in Training (Don't worry. Your elf *will* get killed before you make level 4. It's a rite of passage) you will gain valuable knowledge about the culture and unique personalities that make Gaming what it is.

If you're one of those people who is unfortunate/lucky enough to be a non-gamer dating a gamer, you're *really* lucky: after reading this, you'll understand exactly why your beloved needed to have all three Lord of the Rings DVD sets, buys two of every graphic novel and only reads one, refers to George Lucas as The Great Betrayer, and has 500 pounds of unpainted lead figures safely tucked away in a cardboard box in the garage. Though you will probably not understand why he has several T-shirts from thinkgeek.com, you'll at least understand *why* he needs them, and why he gave you a card for your anniversary that said, in part, "#<include loving_message.h>"

You'll also understand why you must never, ever, under any circumstances, touch his or her dice. I mean that. Don't ever come between a Gamer and their dice. And for the love of god, don't suggest that those people who dress up in animal suits are "cute." They are not. Trust me.

If you've read the previous Dork Tower collections, the following will look very familiar. It's the paragraph where the writer tries to impart to the reader just how goddamn cool John Kovalic is. It's standard to say a few kind words about the author of the work you're introducing, but

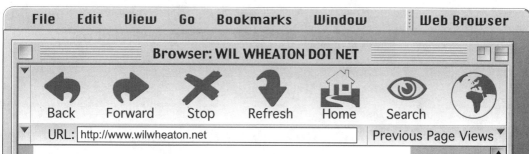

when talking about John, it goes much, much farther than just a few kind words. John is the most sagelike person I've never met. Can you believe that? We've exchanged tons of e-mails, he blurbed my first book, asked me to write this introduction, and even drew me two Munchkin cards with Wesley Crusher on them -- but I've never had the pleasure of buying John a beer or shaking his hand. John is as generous as he is talented.

With Dork Tower, John has accomplished a remarkable task: he's managed to take archetypes, and make them real people. I *know* Matt -- he's my friend Terry. I *know* Igor (Hell, I've *been* Igor more times than I'd like to admit.) I *know* Ken -- he's my friend Cal. Every single one of my guy friends has dated Kayleigh, and we've all lusted after a Gilly. (Why are goth girls so damn hot? Why do they always date those lamer goth guys?) Finally, there is Carson: Carson is, arguably, The Cool One in the group. Every group has The Cool One. In my group, it's my best friend Darin.

John lets us laugh at some of the stupid things we do (shouting "HUZZAH!" when you find out the soup of the day at Denny's is split pea, anyone?), and validates some of the others (repainting an entire Space Marine unit -- including the Rhino -- because you decided to change your unit's insignia, anyone?) John does all of this, brings us all this laughter, lampoons everything we do, without ever making fun of us once. Because John is One of Us, too: he coined the phrase "never summon anything larger than your head," and put "Soylens Viridis Homines Est" in his e-mail .sig.

Hoping that Matt and Gilly finally make successful "find true love" rolls,

Wil Wheaton
Formerly Known As Wesley Crusher
Currently Known As The Author of Dancing Barefoot
Soon To Be Known As The Guy Who Wrote This Intro
Los Angeles, CA

"PENCIL AND PAPER /n./: an archaic information storage and transmission device that works by depositing smears of graphite on bleached wood pulp. More recent developments in paper-based technology include improved `write-once' update devices which use tiny rolling heads similar to mouse balls to deposit colored pigment. All these devices require an operator skilled at so-called 'handwriting' technique."

— From the Jargon File

"So, how's your campaign going?" Diesel asks a 23-year-old gamer in the store. They discuss the guy's campaign, and he then invites Diesel to participate in an upcoming round, saying, "My buddies will never believe Vin Diesel is into D&D."

— Esquire Magazine, August, 2002

NOW, I REALIZE WE ENDED OUR **LAST** ISSUE ON OUR **BIGGEST**, MOST **SHOCKING** AND UTTERLY **UNEXPECTED** CLIFFHANGER IN THE ENTIRE 18-ISSUE RUN OF DORK TOWER...

A CLIFFHANGER THAT LEFT READERS **STUNNED** AND **CLAMORING** FOR THE NEXT INSTALLMENT.

YES, THAT'S RIGHT: THE "WHAT HAPPENED TO KEN'S DICE AFTER KAYLEIGH TOUCHED THEM" CLIFFHANGER.

THAT'S WHEN IT HIT US: HOW COULD WE DELVE INTO SUBJECTS AS ESOTERIC AS **TACTILE DICE THEORY** WHEN A LARGE PERCENTAGE OF OUR READERSHIP SIMPLY **AREN'T** GAMERS (POOR THINGS).

LET'S FACE IT: AS A GROUP, GAMERS ARE ABOUT AS MISUNDERSTOOD AS THEY GET. WHICH IS WHY WE THOUGHT A LITTLE BIT OF **EXPLANATION** MIGHT BE IN ORDER.

GAMING IS AMONG THE MOST **SOCIAL** ACTIVITIES ON THE PLANET. AND YET GAMERS ARE FREQUENTLY PORTRAYED AS **ANTI-SOCIAL DWEEBS** BY THE MEDIA.

GAMING IS A HOBBY THAT STIMULATES THE IMAGINATION, STRENGTHENS COMMUNICATION SKILLS AND **IGNITES** CREATIVITY, YET MANY STILL DISMISS IT AS A **WASTE OF TIME AND ENERGY**.

SO WE DECIDED TO PUT OUR **BIG** CLIFFHANGER ON HOLD FOR A WHILE, AND EXPLORE THE WORLD OF GAMERS AND GAMING, AS A PUBLIC SERVICE TO OUR READERS.

(BESIDES, WE KNOW HOW THE CLIFFHANGER TURNS OUT ALREADY). TRUST US. IT'S NOT PRETTY...)

WHICH IS WHY WE'D LIKE TO WELCOME YOU TO A **VERY SPECIAL** ISSUE OF **DORK TOWER**. ONE **WE'D** LIKE TO CALL

UNDERSTANDING
GAMERS

(IF WE DIDN'T THINK SCOTT McCLOUD WOULD SUE US...)

THE WORLD OF GAMING AND GAMERS PARALLELS THAT OF COMICS AND COMIC BOOK FANS TO A REMARKABLE EXTENT.

NOTE, TOO, THAT BOTH MARKETS SUFFERED DOWNTURNS IN THE OTHER-WISE BOOM ECONOMY OF THE 1990s. BOTH SURVIVED DISTRIBUTOR SHAKEUPS AND COLLECTIBILITY FADS THAT BROUGHT IN MORE SPECULATORS THAN IT DID TRUE FANS.

SIMILARITIES

Comic Book Geeks	Gamer Geeks
Follow their favorite comic book titles religiously.	Follow their favorite game systems religiously.
Collect obscure "in-joke" comic book t-shirts.	Collect obscure "in-joke" gaming t-shirts.
Spend far too much money on their hobby.	Spend far too much money on their hobby.
Liked the live-action "Tick" but LOVED the cartoon.	Grudgingly tolerate the "D&D" movie but LOVED the cartoon.
Revel in extra action figures and comic character lunchboxes.	Revel in extra dice.
Think it's cool that Kevin Smith is a fanboy.	Think it's cool that Robin Williams is a gamer
Know a disturbing number of facts about John Byrne.	Know a disturbing amount on the ecology of the Beholder.
Are mocked by the media.	Are mocked by the media.
Support tired hack creators who are long since past their prime.	Support John Kovalic

YET MUCH MISUNDERSTANDING STILL EXISTS BETWEEN THESE ALTERNATE FANNISH UNIVERSES. THE "ROGUE GAMERS" WHO TAKE THEIR ROLEPLAYING TOO FAR IN THE COMIC BOOK "POWERS," FOR EXAMPLE.

HOW DIFFERENT WERE THEY FROM THE TWO-DIMENSIONAL GAMER STEREOTYPES HOLLYWOOD HAS BEEN GIVING US FOR YEARS?

A SHAME, REALLY, SINCE COMICS FANS AND GAMERS HAVE FAR MORE IN COMMON THAN NOT.

POWERS ROLEPLAY

DIFFERENCES	
Comic Book Geeks	Gamer Geeks
Tend to purchase size M to XL DORK TOWER T-shirts.	Tend to purchase size XL to XXXXL DORK TOWER T-shirts.

CONSIDERING THAT GAMERS TAKE SO MUCH ABUSE AND RIDICULE FROM THE WORLD AT LARGE, YOU MIGHT THINK GAMERS WOULD GO OUT OF THEIR WAY TO BE **TOLERANT** OF OTHERS.

AND THEY DO.

THE ONLY THING GAMERS **CAN'T** STAND IS **OTHER** GAMERS.

DEVIANT...

FREAK...

The Spectrum of Gaming Derision

Historical Gamers mock and distrust Roleplayers.

Roleplayers mock and distrust Live-Action Roleplayers.

Live-Action Roleplayers mock and distrust Card Gamers.

Card Gamers mock and distrust Furries.

HEY! WHO SAID THAT?

WELL, OK. MAYBE THAT LAST ONE'S A BIT MISLEADING.

EVERYBODY MOCKS AND DISTRUSTS FURRIES.

HEY! HEY! **HEY!**

BUT IS THIS THE BEST WAY TO CLASSIFY GAMERS, OR DO THEY FALL INTO **OTHER** AREAS OF CATEGORIZATION?

IN THE 1980s, AARON ALLSTON CREATED A LIST OF GAMERS THAT DIVIDED THEM **NOT** BY THE **GAME TYPE** THEY PLAYED, BUT BY THE **STYLE OF PLAY** THEY ENGAGED IN.

SUCH LISTS HAVE BEEN MODIFIED AND ADAPTED BY OTHERS OVER THE YEARS, BUT HERE ARE A FEW OF THE **MAIN GAMER TYPES** YOU'RE LIKELY TO SEE:

THE THINKER

MOTIVATION: Outwitting the Game Master, outwitting the villain, outwitting traps, outwitting dungeons, outwitting monsters, outwitting ANYBODY.

THE THINKER'S CHARACTER WILL DIE: Violently. Game Masters HATE being outwitted.

AH, BUT HE IS A CUNNING VILLAIN... WE MUST PLAN OUR ATTACK CAREFULLY, MAKING SURE WE MAKE NO MISTAKES HE COULD EXPLOIT. HE'S FAR TOO CLEVER TO...

GOT HIM. I HIT HIM WITH A BRICK...

EVERY DAY, IN EVERY WAY, I WILL BE THE BEST ONE-ARMED, BUCK-TOOTHED LEPROUS HALFLING THIEF WITH A BUM LEG I CAN BE...

THE CHAMP

MOTIVATION: Creating a character who is the absolute best at what they do, be they a fighter, wizard, cleric, chartered accountant...

THE CHAMP'S CHARACTER WILL DIE: Slain by another chartered accountant, who hates being second-best.

THE ACTOR

MOTIVATION: The play's the thing! The Actor looks for acting, storytelling and drama in the game, and would wear tights if it didn't look too ...well...you know...uh...um...yeah...

THE ACTOR'S CHARACTER WILL DIE: In poverty, alone and unloved, the way most actors do.

ALAS POOR FRODO...

LORD, WHAT FOOLS THESE MORTALS BE...

IT'S NOT THE LOOPHOLE IN THE CHARACTER CREATION RULES I MIND... IT'S THE FACT THAT IGOR NOTICED THEM FIRST...

THE MUNCHKIN

MOTIVATION: Exploiting each and every rule to create a wildly improbable yet powerful character every time, then twisting the rules as far as they'll go to become as close to invincible as possible.

THE MUNCHKIN'S CHARACTER WILL DIE: To the delight of everybody.

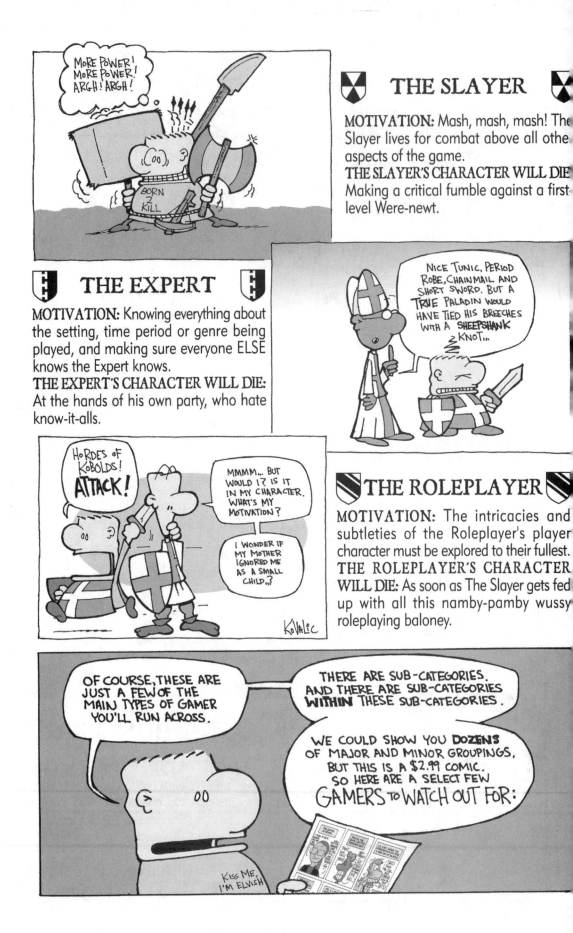

THE SLAYER

MOTIVATION: Mash, mash, mash! The Slayer lives for combat above all other aspects of the game.
THE SLAYER'S CHARACTER WILL DIE: Making a critical fumble against a first-level Were-newt.

THE EXPERT

MOTIVATION: Knowing everything about the setting, time period or genre being played, and making sure everyone ELSE knows the Expert knows.
THE EXPERT'S CHARACTER WILL DIE: At the hands of his own party, who hate know-it-alls.

THE ROLEPLAYER

MOTIVATION: The intricacies and subtleties of the Roleplayer's player character must be explored to their fullest.
THE ROLEPLAYER'S CHARACTER WILL DIE: As soon as The Slayer gets fed up with all this namby-pamby wussy roleplaying baloney.

Everything I Needed to Know I Learned From

GAMING

- YOU CAN'T MAKE A SILK PURSE OUT OF A SOW'S EAR, BUT CROWN ROYAL BAGS ARE COOLER FOR KEEPING DICE ANYWAY.

- BEAUTY IS IN THE EYE OF THE BEHOLDER. UNFORTUNATELY THE REST OF THE PARTY IS IN THE **STOMACH** OF THE BEHOLDER.

- BELIEVE ONLY HALF OF WHAT YOU SEE AND NOTHING OF WHAT YOU HEAR SINCE YOU ALWAYS BLOW YOUR "SPOT HIDDEN" AND "LISTEN" ROLLS.

- NEVER SUMMON ANYTHING BIGGER THAN YOUR HEAD.

- HE WHO FIGHTS AND RUNS AWAY NEVER COULD HAVE GOTTEN AWAY WITH THAT UNDER **SECOND** EDITION RULES.

- A GEM OF SEEING IS BELIEVING.

- DON'T CUT OFF YOUR NOSE TO SPITE YOUR FACE, UNLESS YOUR NAME IS "VECNA."

- IF AT FIRST YOU DON'T SUCCEED, TRY, TRY, TRY REROLLING AGAIN, AND HOPE THE GM DIDN'T NOTICE.

- YOU CAN'T ALWAYS GET WHAT YOU WANT. ESPECIALLY ON PIZZA, WHEN THE ENTIRE GROUP ORDERS.

- DON'T SWEAT THE SMALL STUFF. GNOMES, FOR EXAMPLE.

- A ROD OF SILENCE MEANS NEVER HAVING TO SAY YOU'RE SORRY.

WARHAMSTER ROLEPLAY

XXVII EDITION

SUPER SOAKER

WILL GAME FOR FOOD

PIZZA

CROWN ROYAL

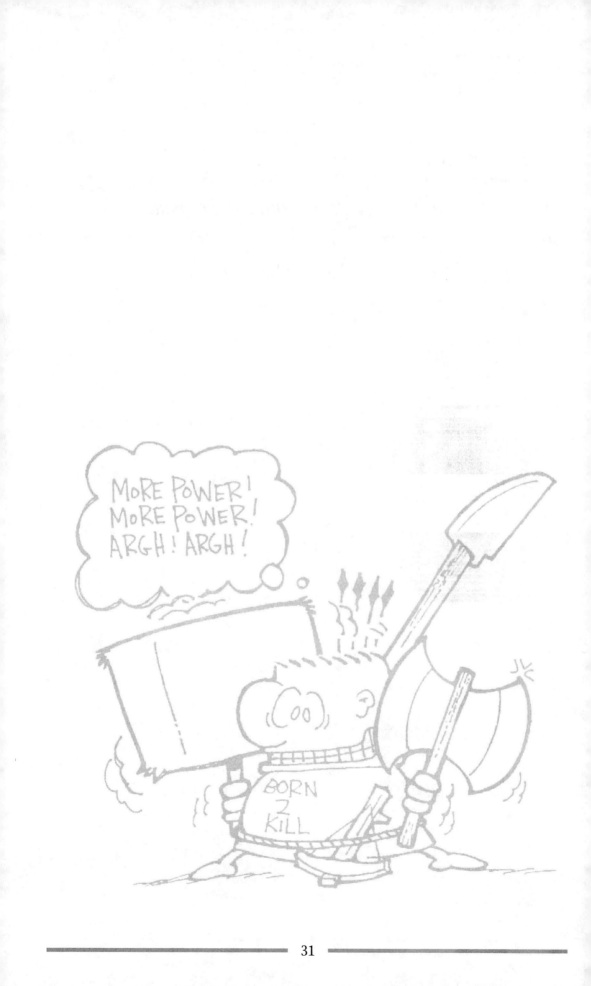

"The Internet? Is that thing still around?"

— Homer Simpson

DORK TOWER.COM

gamespy.com

DORK TOWER

BY JOHN KOVALIC

DORK TOWER

BY JOHN KOVALIC

IN AN OBSCURE CONDO JUST OFF OF SUNSET BOULEVARD, A SECRET SOCIETY OF SELECT INDIVIDUALS GATHERS...

VIN DIESEL – ACTION SUPERSTAR AND CONFIRMED **DUNGEONS AND DRAGONS** PLAYER!

ROBIN WILLIAMS – ACTOR, COMEDIAN AND GAMES WORKSHOP **WARHAMMER** PLAYER!

CURT SCHILLING – WORLD SERIES WINNER AND **ADVANCED SQUAD LEADER** PLAYER AND FINANCER!

...AND **WIL WHEATON** – ACTOR, BLOGGER AND GAMING GEEK! YES, ONCE MORE, IT'S A MEETING OF...

THE LEAGUE OF EXTRAORDINARY GENTLEGAMERS!

STOP TOUCHING MY FREAKING **DICE**, WHEATON!

BITE ME, MORK!

TO BE CONTINUED...

DORK TOWER

BY JOHN KOVALIC

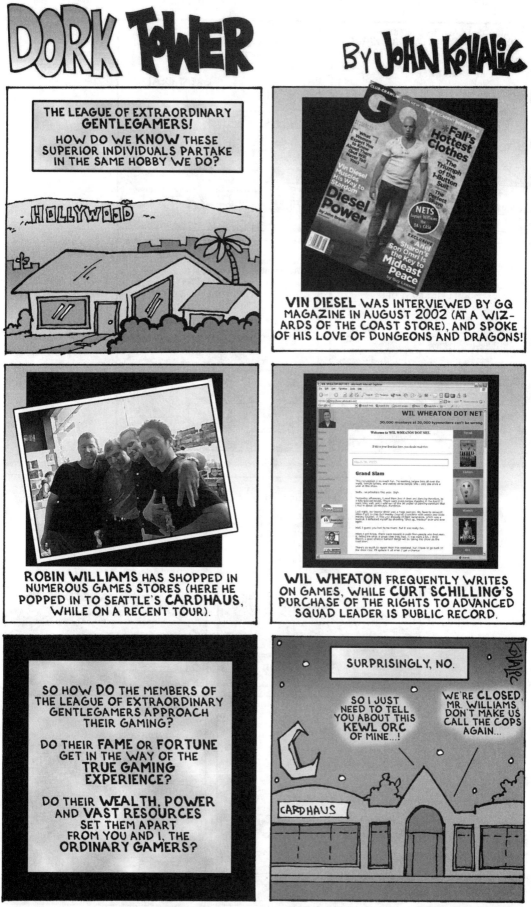

THE LEAGUE OF EXTRAORDINARY GENTLEGAMERS!

HOW DO WE **KNOW** THESE SUPERIOR INDIVIDUALS PARTAKE IN THE SAME HOBBY WE DO?

VIN DIESEL WAS INTERVIEWED BY GQ MAGAZINE IN AUGUST 2002 (AT A WIZARDS OF THE COAST STORE), AND SPOKE OF HIS LOVE OF DUNGEONS AND DRAGONS!

ROBIN WILLIAMS HAS SHOPPED IN NUMEROUS GAMES STORES (HERE HE POPPED IN TO SEATTLE'S **CARDHAUS**, WHILE ON A RECENT TOUR).

WIL WHEATON FREQUENTLY WRITES ON GAMES, WHILE **CURT SCHILLING'S** PURCHASE OF THE RIGHTS TO ADVANCED SQUAD LEADER IS PUBLIC RECORD.

SO HOW **DO** THE MEMBERS OF THE LEAGUE OF EXTRAORDINARY GENTLEGAMERS APPROACH THEIR GAMING?

DO THEIR **FAME** OR **FORTUNE** GET IN THE WAY OF THE **TRUE GAMING EXPERIENCE?**

DO THEIR **WEALTH, POWER** AND **VAST RESOURCES** SET THEM APART FROM YOU AND I, THE ORDINARY GAMERS?

SURPRISINGLY, NO.

SO I JUST NEED TO TELL YOU ABOUT THIS KEWL ORC OF MINE...!

WE'RE **CLOSED**, MR. WILLIAMS. DON'T MAKE US CALL THE COPS AGAIN...

CARDHAUS

TO BE CONTINUED...

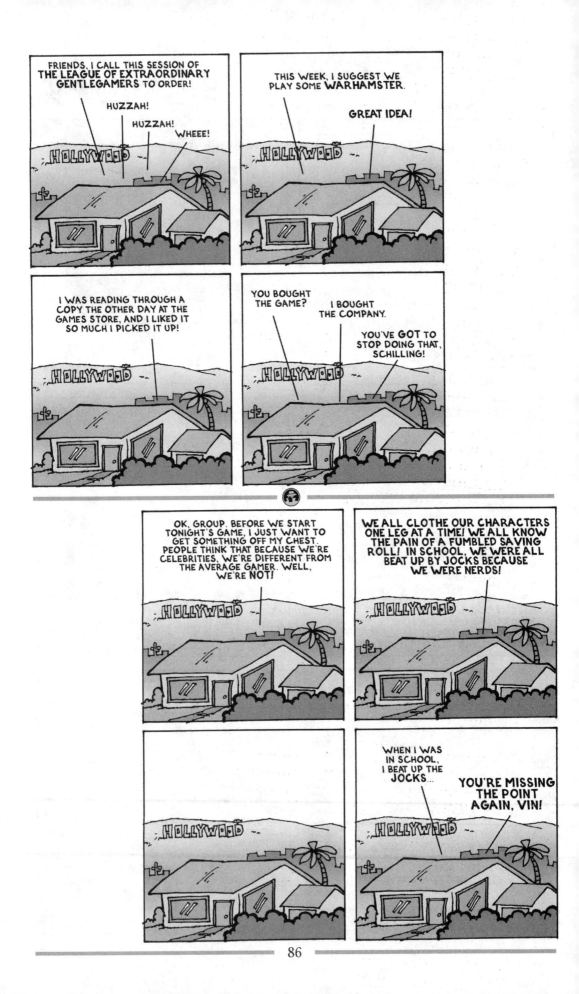

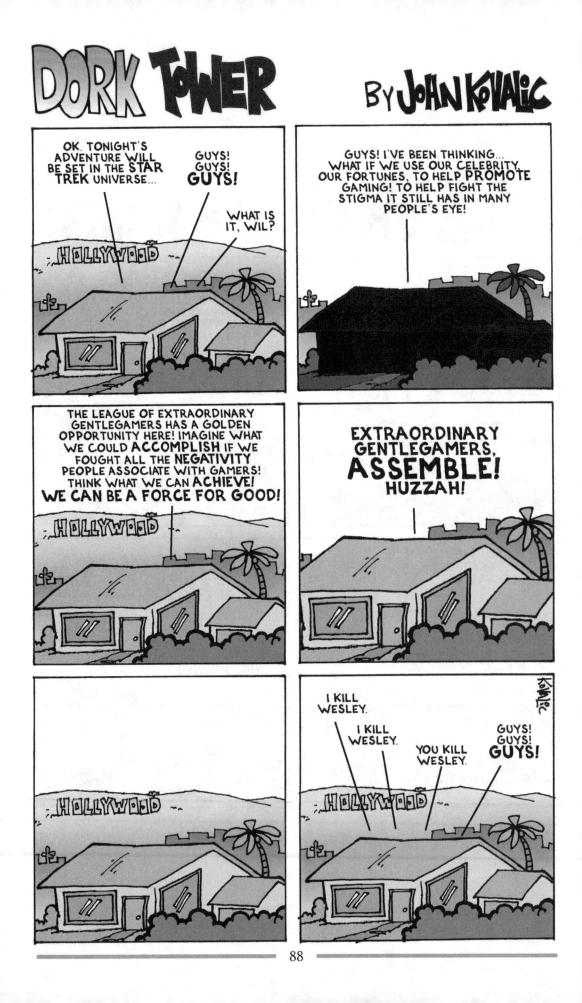

"Peter Adkison, founder of Wizards (of the Coast) and a cherubic visionary...imagined a better, more goblin-infested world where gamers played games and no one gave them wedgies."

— John Tynes, salon.com

SCRYE
THE GUIDE TO COLLECTIBLE CARD GAMES

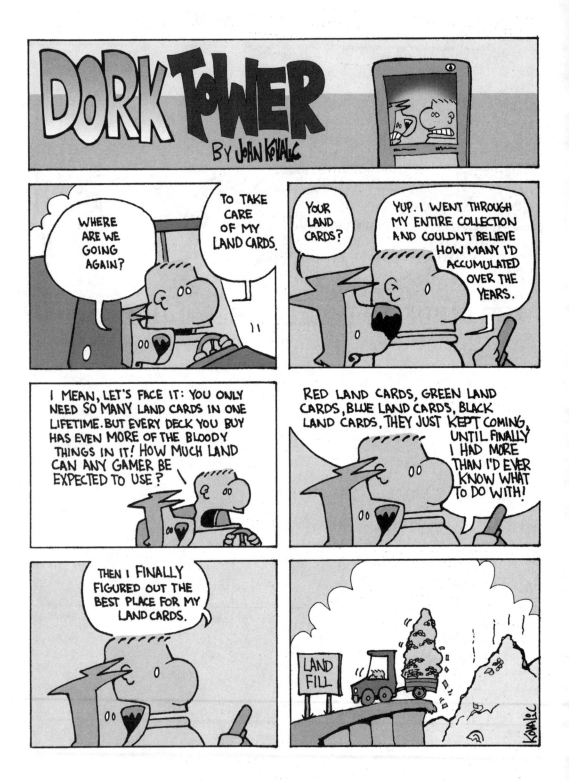

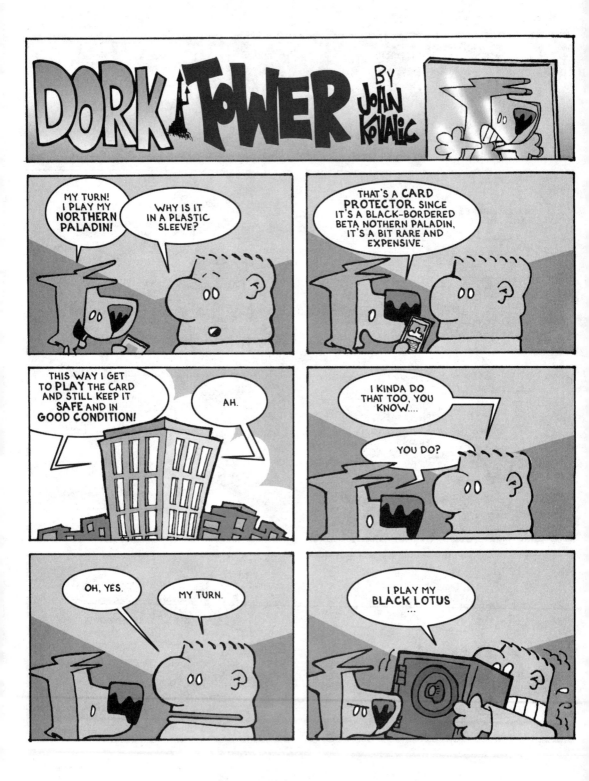

"How far can you bear me?" I said to Gwaihir.
"Many leagues", said he."

— Gandalf, The Lord of the Rings

119

MUSKRAT LOVE

Afterward by Megan Morrone

I have always considered myself an "F-List" celebrity. If Jennifer Lopez is A-List, Jennifer Aniston is B-List, Jennifer Garner is C-List, Jennifer Love-Hewitt is D-List, and Jennifer Ringly (of Jennicam) is E-List, then I am F-List. I'm a sidekick on a cable television show about technology. And my name isn't even Jennifer.

But on January 15th, 2002 something happened that forever changed my life. A Muskrat fell in love with me. I'm not just talking about any Muskrat. I'm talking about Carson the Muskrat, from the wildly popular A-List online comic strip Dork Tower. Back then I wasn't a regular reader of Dork Tower, but many of the people who watch "The Screen Savers" (the cable television show I mentioned above) on TechTV were. Pretty soon after the comic went live on the Web, the emails started pouring in.

To: megan@techtv.com
From: anonymousgeek@linuxrocksmyworld.com
Re: Muskrat Love

Dear Megan,
Carson loves you.

Signed,
Anonymous Geek

To: anonymousgeek@linuxrocksmyworld.com
From: megan@techtv.com
Re: Re: Muscrat Love

Dear AG,
Carson Daly?
I hope not, because I find him kind of annoying.

Yours,
Megan Morrone

It wasn't until people started sending me the link to the comic that I began to understand how important January 15th, 2002 would be in my life. It turns out that Carson the Muskrat had developed a small crush on me. At first I thought it was bizarre, but as I read through the Dork Tower archives, I was impressed. And although I've never admitted this to anyone before, I developed a little crush on Carson. Is it any surprise, considering we have so much in common? We're both geeks. We both hold a special place in our hearts for video games. We're both the sidekicks in our respective media. We're both short. And we both have a lot of hair on our arms.

After January 15th, Carson expressed his love for me in two different strips. But it wasn't until he wrote me a special valentine rhyming my last name with my favorite shellfish (Abalone) that I realized the one tragic obstacle in our relationship. Abalone rhymes with Morrone and Morrone is my married name. Choosing my married name as the centerpiece to his valentine meant that Carson probably had no idea that I was married.

I still don't know if Carson knows I'm married. If he does, I don't think he's really ready to admit it to himself. Muskrat's are that way. They just block things out. I know that there have been a lot of rumors in the press lately about the fact that the baby I'm carrying is, in fact, Carson's. I simply refuse to comment on that.

What I can comment on is John Kovalic's talent and humor which you're no doubt acquainted with having gotten this far in his book. He makes us all laugh and for that reason we should send him nice things or money.

Megan Morrone
Tech TV, The Screen Savers
San Francisco, CA

1d6 Degrees of
SEPARATION
The collected Dork Tower, Volume VI

Compiling Dork Tower #19-24
Autumn, 2003

ABOUT THIS VOLUME

Understanding Gamers is a companion volume to "Livin' La Vida Dorka: The Collected Dork Tower Volume IV," inasmuch as it's a compilation of comic strips outside the "regular" run of Dork Tower comic books. There's no Matt/Gilly/Kayleigh triangle here: just some stuff I had fun with, for the heck of it.

Dork Tower #18 (the original "Understanding Gamers") was one of the best-received comics out of the whole Dork Tower line, even if it has next to nothing to do with the main story arcs in the comic book. There will be a sequel at some point in time ("Understanding Gamers II?" "Reinventing Gamers?"), because there are tons of targets -- uh, sorry, I meant *topics* -- out there that the original comic book didn't have room for.

The Dork Tower Lord of the Rings Special was the best-selling issue of the comic book to this point. It's been translated into German, French, Italian, Spanish and Portuguese meaning that, if nothing else, the phrase "I kill Gandalf" can now derail roleplaying sessions worldwide. The first two stories in the special appeared in other Dork Tower collections, but I've left them in here for the sake of completeness.

What can I say about the rest of the strips? The Scrye series still ranks among my most obscure work for a general audience to try and fathom. As a rule, I try and write Dork Tower so that it can be understood by both Gamers and Non-Gamers alike. But collectible card and clicky-base gaming is what Scrye is about, so here are the strips, in all of their niche-market glory.

I'd like to thank both Wil Wheaton and Megan Morrone (two *great* folks) for their patience and good humor in the GameSpy strips. In fact, Wil and I have a game lined up in July, since we'll both be at San Diego ComiCon. So any revenge that needs be extracted can come in the form of a no-holds barred game of Munchkin.

The next Dork Tower compilation, "1d6 Degrees of Separation," will get back to collecting the Dork Tower comic books. But I hope you've enjoyed "Livin' La Vida Dorka" and "Understanding Gamers" as a quirky change of pace!

— John

About the Author

John Kovalic was born in Manchester, England in 1962, although he's carefully cultivated a Wisconsin accent in the last few years. USA TODAY called the Madison resident a "Hot Pick," and his award-winning cartoons have appeared everywhere from Dragon magazine to the NEW YORK TIMES and the WASHINGTON POST.

The five-time Origins award-winning Dork Tower comic book was launched in June 1998, with its first issue selling out within a matter of weeks. "Dork Tower may just be the perfect comic book," raved Diamond Comics Distributors. Dork Tower is now printed in German, Italian, Portuguese, Spanish, and French editions, proving geekdom is universal.

John was a co-founder and is Art Director of Out of the Box Games (where he's worked on such massive hits as Games Magazine's 1999 Party Game of the Year, "Apples to Apples," among many other award-winning games), and his artwork has graced smashes such as Chez Greek and Munchkin. Along with his SnapDragons partner Liz Rathke, John's warped creations can now be found on WizKids' Creepy Freaks game.

In 2003, John became the first cartoonist ever inducted into the Academy of Adventure Gaming Arts and Design Hall of Fame. Also that year, he created the party quiz game "Whad'Ya Know?" for Out of the Box.

John's degree was in Economics with a minor in Astrophysics. He's never used either. But if you ask him nicely, he may even tell you how he once ended up in the pages of the National Enquirer.

In his spare time, John searches for spare time.